WORKING IN A WOMAN'S WORLD

By Lisa Cofield
Debbie Dingerson
Maia Lacher
Lea Rush

0 43422 69565 2

Written by Debbie Dingerson, Lisa Cofield, Lea Rush
and Maia Lacher
Cover Illustration by Market Force, Burr Ridge, IL
Typography by Dmitry Feygin

Published by Great Quotations Publishing Co.,
Glendale Heights, IL

ISBN 1-56245-277-0

Library of Congress Catalog Card Number: 96-078979

Printed in Hong Kong

Table of contents:

Section 1

In the Classified Ads

So you've decided to get a new job. You start by perusing the ads in the Sunday paper. To help decipher what the ads really mean, we've included a translation guide that lists commonly-used phrases and their true meanings.

"CALL FOR CONFIDENTIAL INTERVIEW"

We're trying to hire the current employees of our closest competitors.

–5–

"SELF-MOTIVATOR"

The pay sure won't be an incentive.

"WORKS WELL INDEPENDENTLY"

You will be stuck in a windowless office alone. Beware of use with "willing to relocate." The office may be in Antarctica.

"TEAM PLAYER / BE A PART OF THE TEAM"

Get none of the credit and all of the blame.

"COMPANY CAR PROVIDED"

Your job will be spent on the road.

"NEED A QUICK THINKER"

You'll be put on the spot daily.

"CUTTING EDGE COMPANY"

We're hoping to find a market for our product.

"OPPORTUNITY TO EXPAND"

We will give you more work. Not to be confused with "opportunity to advance."

"PROFESSIONAL OFFICE ENVIRONMENT"

Suit and/or pumps required.

"EQUAL OPPORTUNITY EMPLOYER"

We exploit everyone equally.

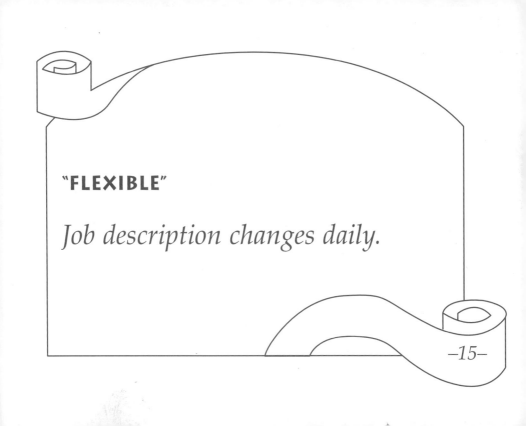

"FLEXIBLE"

Job description changes daily.

"SOME LIFTING REQUIRED"

And it will be one of the few occasions when you're wearing a skirt and high heels.

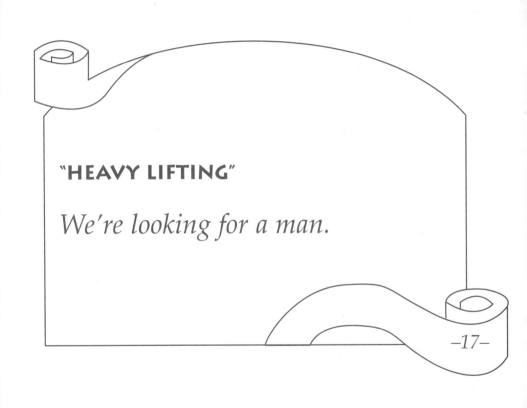

"HEAVY LIFTING"

We're looking for a man.

"EARN A SIX FIGURE SALARY"

Includes the numbers on both sides of the decimal point.

"EXCELLENT CUSTOMER SERVICE SKILLS"

Our top client is really annoyed with us right now.

"GOOD PAY"

No benefits.

"MOTIVATED AND AMBITIOUS"

We will tease you endlessly with the vague possibility of promotion.

"NEED RELIABLE TRANSPORTATION"

Be prepared to make deliveries for the company.

"EARN UP TO $XX,XXX"

Only the veteran employee of forty years makes this much.

"BASE PLUS COMMISSION"

The original salary will barely cover the cost of thank-you notes to your commission clients.

"MUST BE WILLING TO RELOCATE"

If you want to move up, the position won't be here.

"MUST BE WILLING TO TRAVEL"

Kiss your homelife good-bye.

"STAFF AWARE OF SEARCH"

Nobody in the office wants this job.

"NO PHONE CALLS, PLEASE"

We don't think anyone in the office is qualified, and we haven't fired the current job-holder yet.

"FAX RESUME"

Please hurry; we're desperate.

"FEES PAID"

We haven't been able to find a qualified applicant, and we're really, really desperate.

"PROFIT SHARING"

We can't pay you a decent wage now, but we will if the company ever becomes financially solvent.

**"CAREER-ORIENTED
INDIVIDUAL WANTED"**

*Willing to put the company needs
before self, family, country...*

"DETAIL-ORIENTED"

We need someone to help sort the stack of stuff left behind by the last person.

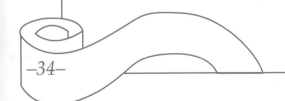

"EXPERIENCE WANTED"

Of course, you can't get any experience until someone hires you.

"NO EXPERIENCE NECESSARY"

We'll hire you even if you can't walk and chew gum at the same time.

"COMPENSATION TIME AVAILABLE"

Lots of unpaid overtime.

"GOOD RETIREMENT PLAN"

The better it sounds, the less likely anyone can stick with the job long enough to collect.

"OPPORTUNITY TO WORK AT HOME"

The job can't be completed in forty hours a week.

"EAGER/ENTHUSIASTIC"

Must be gullible enough to do the jobs nobody else wants to do.

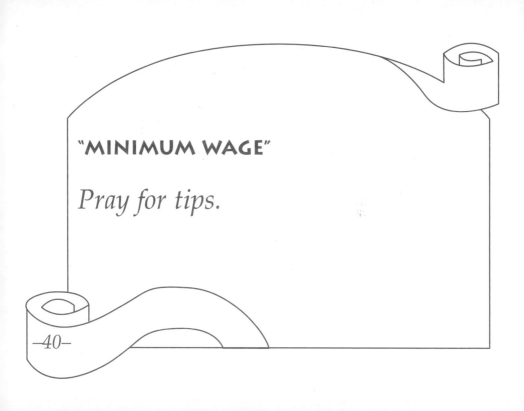

"MINIMUM WAGE"

Pray for tips.

"FLEXIBLE HOURS"

Swing shift and weekend work will be required.

"GOOD COMMUNICATION SKILLS"

You'll have to repeat yourself due to the surrounding poor listening skills.

"GOOD PEOPLE PERSON"

Everyone here is a jerk.

"GOOD SENSE OF HUMOR"

The boss tells tasteless jokes.

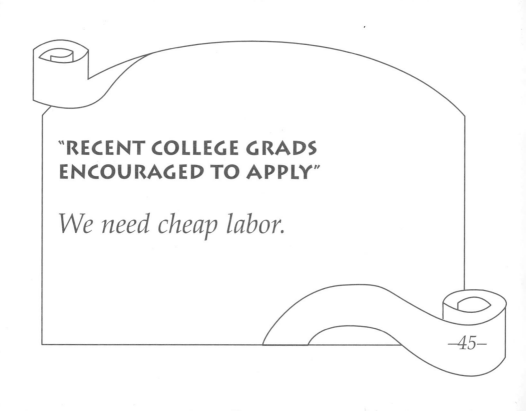

"RECENT COLLEGE GRADS ENCOURAGED TO APPLY"

We need cheap labor.

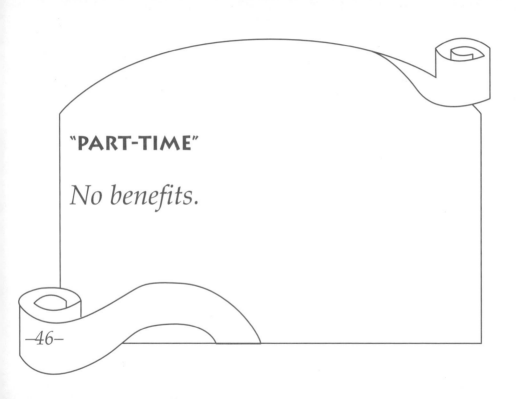

"PART-TIME"

No benefits.

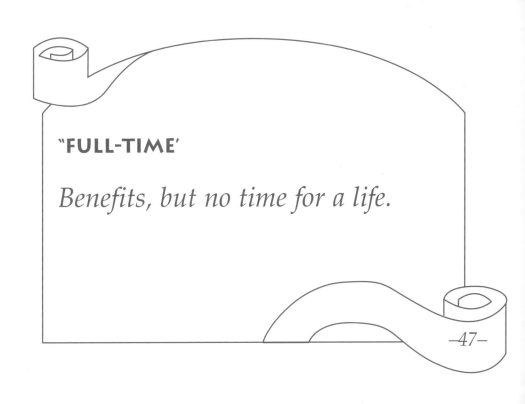

"FULL-TIME'

Benefits, but no time for a life.

"SALARIED POSITION"

Averages 50 to 60 hours per week with no overtime pay.

"FAMILY-OWNED BUSINESS"

No union sympathizers, please.

–49–

"ON-SITE FITNESS FACILITY"

We provide a healthy alternative to "happy hour."

"DAYCARE ON-SITE"

A place where you discover the behavior of our children is not that much different from the behavior of your co-workers.

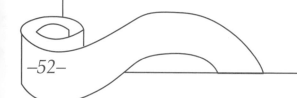

"LONG-TERM TEAM PLAYER"

Please stay longer than six months.

"E-MAIL RESUME"

We are looking for people with Internet experience.

"INCOME UNLIMITED"

The pay is 100% commission, 0% base salary.

"EXCELLENT REFERENCES REQUIRED"

Former employee was escorted from the premises by security.

"IMMEDIATE OPENING"

Former employee left with no notice.

"CALL OUR JOBLINE FOR MORE INFO"

Our budget is too small to place a full ad.

"COMPUTER SKILLS REQUIRED"

We're looking for someone to show us where the "on" switch is.

"PROVEN PERFORMERS NEEDED IMMEDIATELY"

Our cash flow is in real trouble.

"PROBLEM-SOLVING SKILLS REQUIRED"

... and boy, do we have problems.

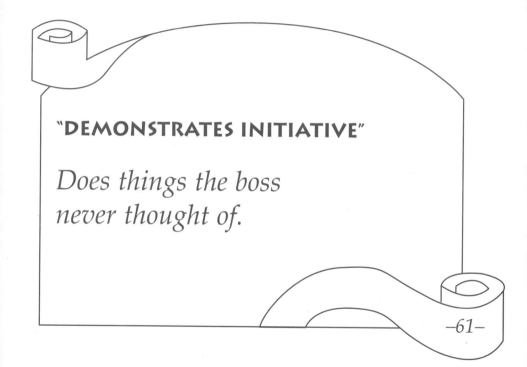

"DEMONSTRATES INITIATIVE"

*Does things the boss
never thought of.*

"FREE PARKING"

This is the only benefit we can advertise.

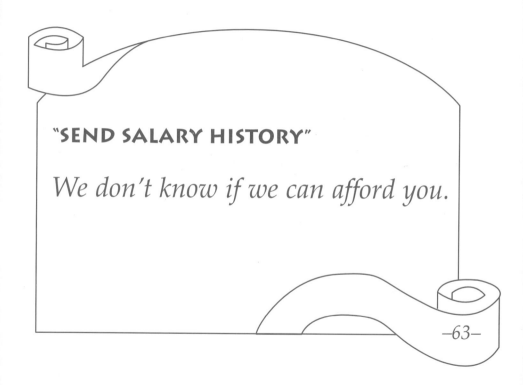

"SEND SALARY HISTORY"

We don't know if we can afford you.

"MUST BE ABLE TO REMAIN AWAKE DURING ENTIRE SHIFT"

We certainly hope that this is from an ad for a night job.

"INCENTIVE PROGRAM"

We'll pay you a token fee for coming up with ideas that will make the company millions.

"STRONG NEGOTIATION SKILLS"

You'll be on the unpopular side of a labor strike.

"FAST-PACED ENVIRONMENT"

Be prepared to have jogging shoes issued at the door.

"MANAGEMENT SKILLS REQUIRED"

Lion-tamer's chair a plus.

Section 2

On the Job

Now that you have a job, you probably have a boss and several co-workers to deal with. Throughout your working day, you'll hear a variety of sometimes vague phrases. Here's what they really mean.

"THE NEXT THREE MONTHS WILL BE CRITICAL."

If we don't make a profit, we'll all lose our jobs.

"WE OFFER EMPLOYEE DISCOUNTS"

We'll help you spend your salary here.

"YOU'LL NEED TO WORK SOME EVENING HOURS"

You'll be working nights until someone with less seniority than you is hired.

**"WE HAVE A BUS PASS
SUBSIDY PROGRAM."**

*There is no parking within 5 miles
of this office.*

"THIS PROJECT IS GOING TO BE ONE OF OUR GREATEST CHALLENGES."

"I don't have the faintest idea how we're going to do this."

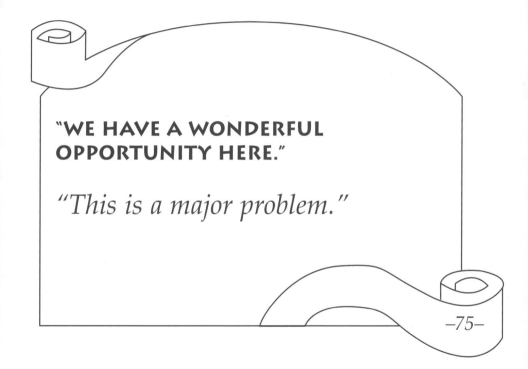

"WE HAVE A WONDERFUL OPPORTUNITY HERE."

"This is a major problem."

–75–

"I'D LIKE TO REACH A CONSENSUS HERE."

"Please rubber-stamp my plan, but take 45 minutes to discuss it."

"THERE ARE SOME THINGS I'D LIKE TO DISCUSS WITH YOU."

"I have no clue what to do about this problem."

"I'M NOT SURE WE'RE COMMUNICATING EFFECTIVELY."

"You still don't agree with me."

"THIS IS NOT COMPANY POLICY."

"The boss doesn't like it, but can't justify why."

"THERE ARE GOING TO BE SOME CHANGES AROUND HERE."

"Somebody has been, or will be, fired."

"**WE NEED TO PICK UP THE PACE.**"

"*Sixty hour weeks from now on.*"

"THE CORPORATION WILL BE RESTRUCTURING."

"You may have noticed that half your colleagues no longer work here."

"WE'D LIKE YOU TO CONSIDER TAKING ON NEW CHALLENGES."

"You're about to be given your colleague's duties in addition to your own."

–83–

"EVERYONE NEEDS TO TAKE MORE RESPONSIBILITY."

"I'm tired of taking all the blame myself."

"WHAT DO YOU THINK WE SHOULD DO?"

"Time for you to think for yourself."

"I'VE GOT IT ALL TAKEN CARE OF."

"I've already delegated it to one of my subordinates."

"WE NEED TO WORK SMARTER, NOT HARDER."

"There's no money in the budget for the overtime pay you're entitled to."

"THAT'S NOT IN THE BUDGET."

"I don't care how indispensable it is, I'm not going to pay for it."

"THAT'S NOT IN THE MISSION STATEMENT."

"I don't deal with new ideas, no matter how good they are."

"THE BOSS IS A PERSON OF VISION."

"The boss's corner office has a 270 degree view."

"WHAT'S YOUR SCHEDULE LIKE?"

"I'm going to assign you a project that will fill all available times.

"COULD YOU STEP INTO MY OFFICE?"
(DOOR OPEN)

"Did you tape last night's episode of 'Friends'?"

"COULD YOU STEP INTO MY OFFICE?"
(DOOR CLOSED)

"I have some bad news..."

"UPGRADE? WHY DO WE NEED AN UPGRADE?"

"This software has been working fine for the past 7 years."

"FULLY VESTED AFTER FIVE YEARS"

"After ten years, you can afford the rest of the suit."

"COMPANY OF LONG-STANDING TRADITION"

"Run by stodgy old men who believe that women are only good for decoration and shorthand."

"CASUAL FRIDAYS" (DRESS-DOWN DAYS)

No-one is quite certain whether this means "denim jeans OK" or simply "no tie or pumps required."

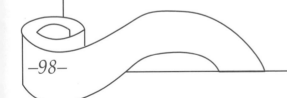

MANDATORY ATTENDANCE

If you don't show up, you'll be assigned to a committee.

"WOULD YOU LIKE TO GO ON A BUSINESS TRIP?"

"You get to go to an exotic location but only see the inside of a conference room."

"WE'RE UNDER A DEADLINE HERE."

The boss has known about it for 3 weeks, but lets you know the night before."

LEVELS OF URGENCY

Priority - It's for a client
Urgent - It's for the boss's boss
Imperative - It's for the boss's spouse
Critical - It's for the boss's in-laws

"WE NEED TO RE-ENGINEER THE COMPANY."

"Things are really off track."

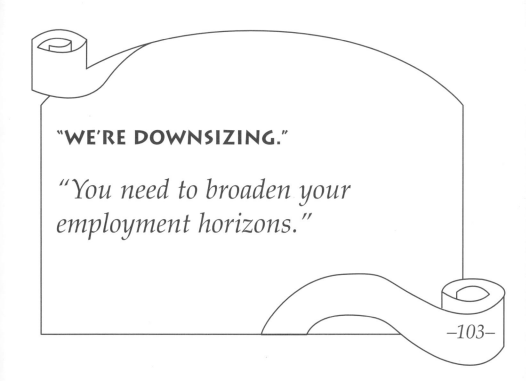

"WE'RE DOWNSIZING."

"You need to broaden your employment horizons."

–103–

"I'D LIKE TO HELP YOU GAIN MORE VISIBILITY."

"I need a scapegoat."

"WE NEED TO DEVELOP A CONTINGENCY PLAN."

"We had better cover our backsides on this one."

Section 3

Your Performance Review

After you've been on the job for awhile, it will be time for your first performance review. Depending on the results of the review, you may need a letter of recommendation for another job. Commonly used phrases in both performance reviews and letters of recommendations, and their true meanings, are explained in the next section.

"MAKES APPROPRIATE USE OF FORMAL VS. INFORMAL COMMUNICATIONS"

Knows when to take clients out to lunch.

"MAKES THE BEST IMPRESSION IN ALL SITUATIONS"

Knows the proper use of a power suit.

"DEMONSTRATES SOUND NEGOTIATING SKILLS"

Could engineer a contract with the client from hell.

"COMMUNICATES EFFECTIVELY WITH ALL LEVELS OF MANAGEMENT"

Can suck up to anyone.

**"EXCELS IN OBTAINING
MANAGEMENT SUPPORT
FOR PROJECTS"**

Has major dirt on the boss.

"RESPONDS QUICKLY TO ALL ORAL AND WRITTEN COMMUNICATION"

Speaks and writes before thinking.

"MAKES EFFECTIVE USE OF THE TELEPHONE"

Knows when not to put something in writing.

"POSSESSES EXTENSIVE VOCABULARY"

Can phrase even the most dismal news into positive words.

"IS UNIQUELY QUALIFIED"

We've never had it done quite this way before.

"MAKES EFFECTIVE USE OF STATISTICAL APPLICATIONS"

Makes the sales figures look good.

"PROPERLY CONTROLS THE RELEASE OF PROPRIETARY INFORMATION"

Doesn't talk to the press or the competition.

"RESPECTS CONFIDENTIAL INFORMATION"

Only repeats it in the boss's office with the door closed.

"MAKES EFFECTIVE USE OF OFFICE EQUIPMENT"

Doesn't use the company copier for holiday newsletters to the family.

"DEMONSTRATES A STRONG ABILITY TO ANALYZE PROBLEMS"

Was able to salvage the most important account at the 11th hour.

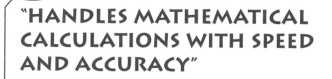

"HANDLES MATHEMATICAL CALCULATIONS WITH SPEED AND ACCURACY"

Is the only person who can deal with the budget.

"USES A VARIETY OF TECHNIQUES TO SOLVE PROBLEMS"

Is willing to try anything to fix a situation.

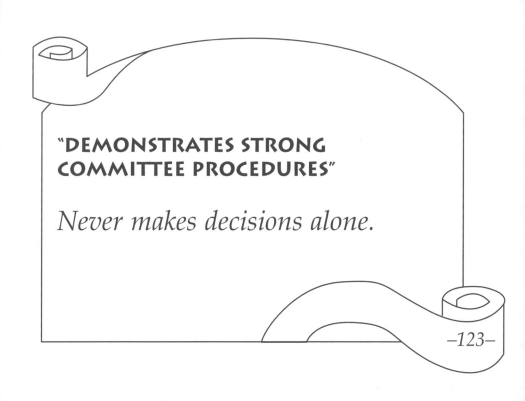

"DEMONSTRATES STRONG COMMITTEE PROCEDURES"

Never makes decisions alone.

"IS SKILLFUL MEETING PARTICIPANT"

Sits in the front row.

"MAKES A STRONG IMPACT AT MEETINGS"

Brings the donuts.

"CONVEYS SINCERE APPRECIATION AT EVERY OPPORTUNITY"

Has a drawer full of blank thank you notes and small gifts.

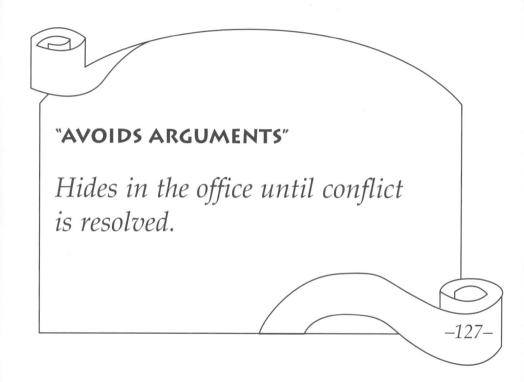

"AVOIDS ARGUMENTS"

Hides in the office until conflict is resolved.

"CLOSELY FOLLOWS ALL OPERATIONAL PROCEDURES"

Can quote the company policy manual chapter and verse.

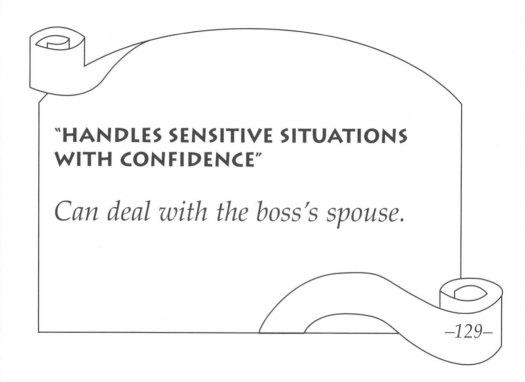

"HANDLES SENSITIVE SITUATIONS WITH CONFIDENCE"

Can deal with the boss's spouse.

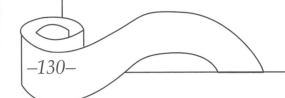

"ENSURES THAT ALL PERSONNEL PROBLEMS ARE PROPERLY DOCUMENTED"

Has 4-inch thick files on everyone.

"TURNS COMPLAINTS INTO OPPORTUNITIES"

Drives co-workers crazy with "Pollyanna" impersonations.

"DEMONSTRATES THE ABILITY TO DEVELOP FROM A SPECIALIST TO A GENERALIST."

Became the company "jack of all trades" in order to keep job.

"EFFECTIVELY DELEGATES UNPLEASANT TASKS"

Is able to give away any job they don't want to do.

"DISPLAYS A STRONG PERSONAL COMMITMENT TO SUCCESSFULLY COMPLETING PROJECTS"

Has no homelife. Sleeps in office and showers in company gym.

"UTILIZES ALL AVAILABLE RESOURCES TO ACHIEVE RESULTS"

This person's Rolodex™ is packed.

"RECOGNIZES THE IMPORTANCE OF ACCURACY"

Really messed up once, but knows better now.

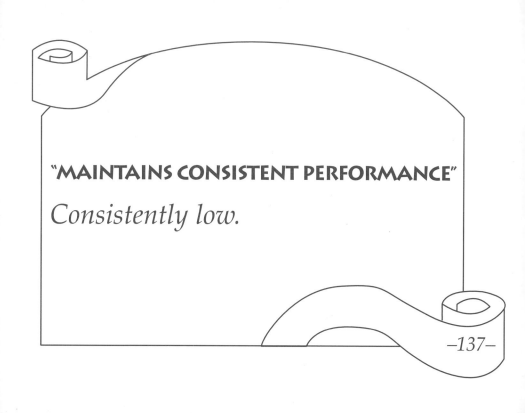

"MAINTAINS CONSISTENT PERFORMANCE"

Consistently low.

"STRIVES FOR PERFECTION"

Drives us all crazy with nitpicky details.

"AVOIDS MISTAKES AND ERRORS"

Because will only attempt simple projects.

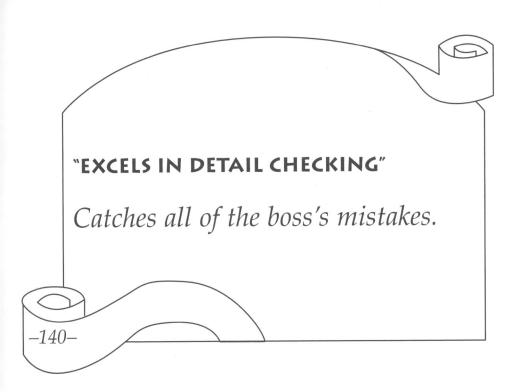

"EXCELS IN DETAIL CHECKING"

Catches all of the boss's mistakes.

–140–

"ACCOMPLISHES MORE WITH FEWER PEOPLE"

We've downsized and this person's department is non-existent.

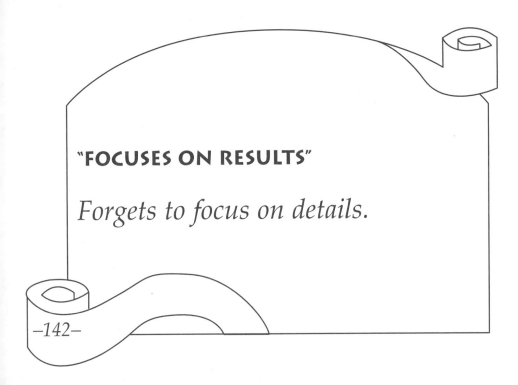

"FOCUSES ON RESULTS"

Forgets to focus on details.

"EXCELS IN REDUCING PAPERWORK"

All data is in this person's head - if she ever leaves, we're toast.

"EFFECTIVELY USES EXCEPTION REPORTING TO KEEP MANAGEMENT INFORMED"

Snitch.

"KEEPS SIMPLE RECORDS WITH LITTLE DUPLICATION"

And we've lost the unduplicated records.

"THOROUGHLY ANALYZES CONDITIONS AND REACHES INDEPENDENT DECISIONS"

Doesn't wait for supervisor's approval.

"EFFECTIVELY HANDLES WORK OVERLOADS"

We promised this person an assistant 6 months ago.

"KEEPS INFORMED OF THE LATEST TRENDS AND DEVELOPMENTS"

Has a subscription to every trade journal in existence.

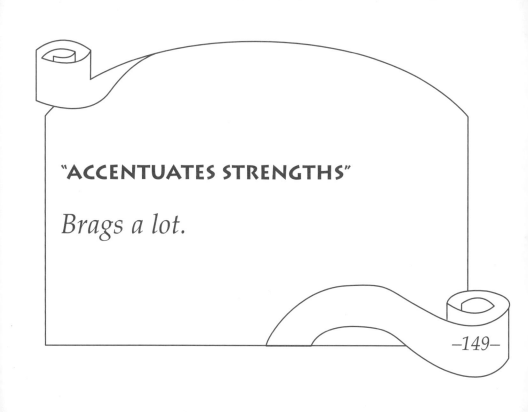

"ACCENTUATES STRENGTHS"

Brags a lot.

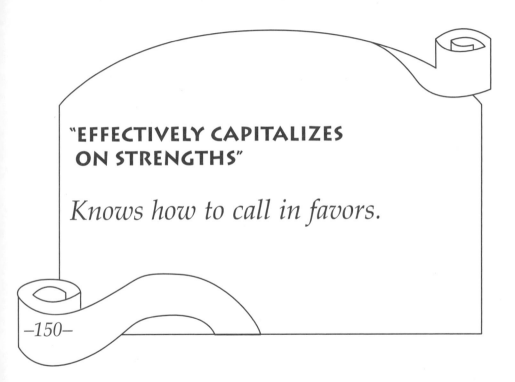

"EFFECTIVELY CAPITALIZES ON STRENGTHS"

Knows how to call in favors.

–150–

"DEALS EFFECTIVELY WITH FISCAL RESTRAINTS"

Can work on a shoestring budget.

"MAINTAINS STRONG SELF-CONTROL"

Does not strangle the client after the 100th change request on a project.

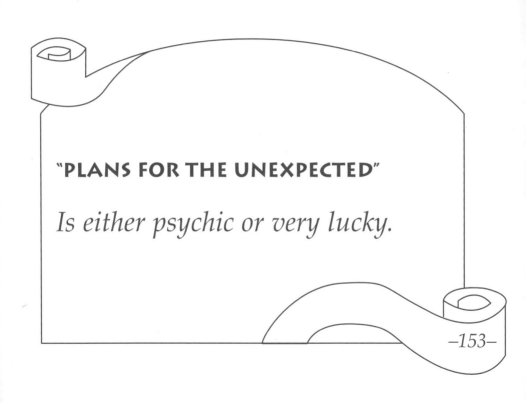

"PLANS FOR THE UNEXPECTED"

Is either psychic or very lucky.

"PERFORMS WELL IN CRISIS SITUATION"

Doesn't hide under desk during company audit.

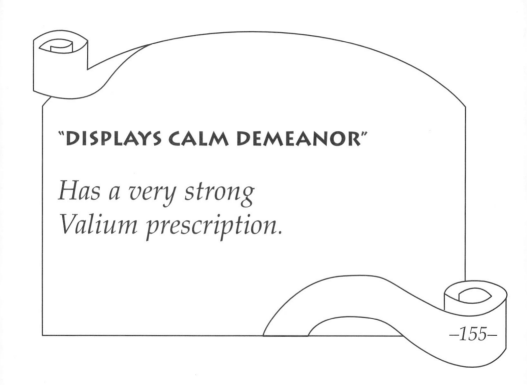

"DISPLAYS CALM DEMEANOR"

Has a very strong Valium prescription.

"COPES EFFECTIVELY WITH RISK AND UNCERTAINTY"

Doesn't mind not knowing where next paycheck will come from.

"BUILDS TEAM SPIRIT"

Former high school cheerleader.

**"MAKES EFFECTIVE USE OF
SECRETARIAL SUPPORT"**

*Can't type with more than
two fingers.*

"MAY BE DELEGATED THE BROADEST DISCRETION"

Does the boss's job, but for a lot less money.

"STRIVES TO IMPROVE DECISIVENESS"

Needs to be told what to do.

"AVOIDS CONFUSING ACTIVITY WITH ACCOMPLISHMENT"

Actually gets a task done.

"MAKES EFFECTIVE USE OF PEAK TIME PERIODS"

Can eat lunch, type a report and make phone calls all at once.

"MAKES EFFECTIVE USE OF DISCRETIONARY TIME"

Does not have trashy romance novel in the top desk drawer.

"MAKES EFFECTIVE USE OF TRAVEL TIME"

Can write a presentation to a client in 45 minutes on the commuter train.

"IDENTIFIES UNESSENTIAL ACTIVITIES"

Still does them, but knows what they are.

"CONCENTRATES ON AREAS THAT YIELD THE GREATEST RETURN"

Knows where the high commissions are.

"RESOLVES TEAM CONFLICTS WITH FINESSE"

Is able to keep co-workers from strangling one another.

Other Titles By Great Quotations

201 Best Things Ever Said
The ABC's of Parenting
As a Cat Thinketh
The Best of Friends
The Birthday Astrologer
Chicken Soup & Other Yiddish Say
Cornerstones of Success
Don't Deliberate ... Litigate!
Fantastic Father, Dependable Dad
Global Wisdom
Golden Years, Golden Words
Grandma, I Love You
Growing up in Toyland
Happiness is Found Along The Way
Hollywords
Hooked on Golf
In Celebration of Women
Inspirations Compelling Food for Thought
I'm Not Over the Hill
Let's Talk Decorating
Life's Lessons
Life's Simple Pleasures
A Light Heart Lives Long
Money for Nothing, Tips for Free

Mother, I Love You
Motivating Quotes for Motivated People
Mrs. Aesop's Fables
Mrs. Murphy's Laws
Mrs. Webster's Dictionary
My Daughter, My Special Friend
Other Species
Parenting 101
Reflections
Romantic Rhapsody
The Secret Language of Men
The Secret Language of Women
Some Things Never Change
The Sports Page
Sports Widow
Stress or Sanity
Teacher is Better than Two Books
Teenage of Insanity
Thanks from the Heart
Things You'll Learn if You Live Long Enough
Wedding Wonders
Working Women's World
Interior Design for Idiots
Dear Mr. President

GREAT QUOTATIONS PUBLISHING COMPANY
1967 Quincy Court
Glendale Heights, IL 60139 - 2045
Phone (630) 582-2800
Fax (630) 582- 2813